C000001090

The Vik

From different points of view

Tim Vicary

Millfield Primary School and
Community Centre
Hat Road
Braunstone
Leicester LE3 2WF
Tel: 0533 897151

Mill...
Com... School and
Ha...
Br...
L...
T...

Oxford University Press 1993

The Vikings

This year we're building a warship.
It's beautiful. We call it *Dragon*.
This summer we'll sail to England in it.

The land here in Norway is stony and poor.
The English people are rich,
and they don't believe we can cross the sea.
We laugh. *Dragon* will slide smoothly through the waves.

An English monk, Alcuin

Peaceful monks were living on an island called Lindisfarne.
But this year the Vikings came.
They jumped out of their ship, waving swords and axes,
and screaming!
They killed the monks. There was blood all over the
church!
They stole the gold, and took men and women as slaves.
Please God, save us from the fury of these men!

The Vikings

It was a good raid. We picked up lots of gold and slaves.
Then we steered our ship back home,
looking at the sun and stars to guide us.

Our families prepared a feast in the great hall.
We're singing songs and telling stories of our Gods.
Next summer, we'll sail east to sell our slaves.

Edith, an English slave

They dragged me from my home, and tied my arms.
They put me in their ship, and I was frightened and cold.
All winter, I had to work outside in the snow.
I slept with the animals.

Now I'm standing in the market like a cow, waiting
to be sold.
I'll never see England, or my family, again!

Ivar the Boneless, a Viking chief

When I was young, the English threw my father into a snake-pit.

Now I am back in England with a large army.
We're going to live here.
We've captured the city of York.

It's a good country, with rich flat fields.
Better than our poor rocky farms at home.
Soon we'll rule the whole of England!

Gytha, a woman of York

My husband is Ragnar, a Viking jeweller.
He makes rings, brooches, and necklaces.
He sells them outside our house.

I make most of our clothes in our house.
First I comb the wool, then I spin it on a spindle.
After that I dye it in bright colours and weave it on our
loom.

Guthrum, a Viking King

We Vikings sail all over the world.
There are Viking kings in many countries.
Now my armies are going to make me king of all
England.

Last winter we chased the English all over Wessex.
Their king is hiding in the marshes somewhere.
He won't last long. Our god Thor will crush him with
his hammer!

Alfred, the English King of Wessex

We came out of the marshes and beat the Vikings.
We were so happy! We carved a white horse on the
hillside.
I baptised the Viking king, Guthrum.

I told the Vikings to stay in the north of England.
But Viking ships still raided the coast.
So I built huge longships, twice as big as theirs.
They didn't like that. We chased them away.

Erik Bloodaxe, Viking King of York

I live in York. It's a fine, rich city for Vikings. Our ships trade all over the world, bringing bright clothes and jewels.

We make chessmen and ice skates out of bone.
I wear a heavy chainmail shirt, to protect me in battle.
My helmet looks fierce and wild.

Ethelred, King of the English

The Vikings have come again. What shall I do?
Last year I paid them to go away,
but now they've come back to ask for more.
Perhaps I made a mistake. What can I do?

Cnut the Viking

Ethelred died, and I married his wife.
My men say even the sea obeys me, but that's nonsense.
They say it because I am King of all England, and
Denmark too!

At first, the Vikings raided England and stole things.
Later, they came to live in the north of England.
Their children grew up half Viking, and half English too.

We still use Viking words today:
words like 'egg', 'take', 'kid', 'skirt' and 'freckle'.
If your village name ends in 'thorpe' or 'by', this shows
that Vikings lived there before you, long ago.

Timeline for the Vikings

793	The Vikings attack Lindisfarne.
867	Ivar the Boneless and his brothers capture York.
878	Guthrum's armies attack Wessex.
886	King Alfred baptises Guthrum.
947–954	Erik Bloodaxe is King of York.
980–994	King Ethelred pays money to the Vikings.
1016–1035	Cnut is the Viking King of all England.

Oxford University Press, Walton Street, Oxford OX2 6DP

Oxford   New York   Toronto
Delhi   Bombay   Calcutta   Madras   Karachi
Kuala Lumpur   Singapore   Hong Kong   Tokyo
Nairobi   Dar es Salaam   Cape Town
Melbourne   Auckland   Madrid

and associated companies in
Berlin   Ibadan

Oxford is a trade mark of Oxford University Press
© Tim Vicary 1993

Illustrations by Victor Ambrus

0 19 917229 3
0 19 917239 0 (pack of 6)

Typeset by Pentacor PLC, High Wycombe, Bucks
Printed in Hong Kong